AIR FRYER COOKING

Making Tasty And Healthy Dishes With The Air Fryer

STEPHANIE SIMMONS

Disclaimer Notice:

Please note the information contained within this document is for educational and entertainment purposes only. All effort has been executed to present accurate, up to date, and reliable, complete information. No warranties of any kind are declared or implied. Readers acknowledge that the author is not engaging in the rendering of legal, financial, medical or professional advice. The content within this book has been derived from various sources. Please consult a licensed professional before attempting any techniques outlined in this book.

By reading this document, the reader agrees that under no circumstances is the author responsible for any losses, direct or indirect, which are incurred as a result of the use of information contained within this document, including, but not limited to, errors, omissions, or inaccuracies.

Table Of Contents

INTRODUCTION

Air fryers work by cooking food with the circulation of hot air. This is what makes the foods you put into it so crispy when they come out! Something called the "Maillard Effect" happens, which is a chemically induced reaction that occurs to the heat that makes it capable for this fryer to brown foods in such a short time, while keeping nutrients and flavor intact.

The Benefits of Using an Air Fryer

A massive reduction in oil –no more than a tsp or two of foil is needed to cook food in an air fryer and yet it still achieves the same texture. A far cry from the many cups of oil that you would have to use to cook food in a deep fryer. The result is food that is not soaked in unhealthy fat that will clog the arteries.

Bursting with flavor – the flavor of the food truly comes out in an air fryer. Despite the small amount of oil used in "frying" the food, the "fried" taste and texture is achieved. Easy press-and-go operation –No longer do you need to watch over your frying pan on your stove while frying your food. This also means no splattering of oil and accidental burns. All of the magic happens in the cooking chamber, just set your cooking preferences, push the right button, and let the air fryer do all of the work.

Rapid cooking times –The high temperatures that are circulated in the cooking chamber cut common cooking times in half. This is because the heat is maintained throughout the time being cooked meaning you do not have to worry about the loss of heat slowing down your cooking.

Cleaning made Easy –With food baskets that are dishwasher safe, it's as simple as removing it and putting it in. The cooking chamber can easily be cleaned with a cloth and a mild dishwashing soap.

Versatile unmatched – this modern appliance is more than just a fryer. You can bake, grill, and broil in it too. More of a highly versatile, mini convection oven rather than a fryer.

Safe – Its components are food safe and the cooking process itself helps you avoid kitchen accidents that can result in oil burns. The body of the air fryer hardly gets hot even if the temperature inside is at its highest. Using your standard kitchen gloves will give you more than enough protection when handling this kitchen appliance.

These benefits make air fryers the obvious choice when it comes to healthy cooking No compromise on flavor or convenience!

To dumb it down, air fryers can do what those oil fryers do, but in a much healthier way than submerging food into greasy and fattening oil.

Getting the Most Out of your Air Fryer

To maximize the benefits of using an air fryer, here are some tips that you should not overlook:

Getting Started

• Place your air fryer on a level and heatproof kitchen top, if you have granite surfaces this is perfect.

• Avoid putting it close to the wall as this will dissipate the heat causing slower cooking times. Leave a space of at least five inches between the wall and the air fryer.

• Oven-safe baking sheets and cake pans may be used in the air fryer on the condition that they can fit inside easily and the door can close.

Before Cooking

• If you can, always preheat your air fryer for 3 minutes before cooking. Once the timer goes off it will be ready to rock and roll.

• Use a hand pumped spray bottle for applying the oil. Adopting this method will cause you to use less oil and is an easier option when compared to brushing or drizzling. Avoid canned aerosol brands as they tend to have a lot of nasty chemicals

• Always Bread if necessary. This breading step should not be missed. Be sure to press the breading firmly onto the meat or vegetable so the crumbs do not fall off easily.

Whilst Cooking

• Adding water to the air fryer drawer while cooking high-fat foods to will prevent excessive smoke and heat. Use this technique when cooking burgers, bacon, sausage and similar foods.

• Secure light foods such as bread slices with toothpicks so they don't get blown around.

• Avoid putting too many food items into the air fryer basket. Overcrowding will result in uneven cooking and will also prevent the food from getting that glorious crispy texture that we all love.

• Shaking the fryer and flipping the food halfway through the cooking process is advised to make sure that everything inside cooks evenly.

• Opening the air fryer a few times to check how the food is doing won't affect the cooking time, so don't worry.

Once done:

• Remove the basket from the drawer before taking out the food to prevent the oil remaining on the food that you just fried.

• The juices in the air fryer drawer can be used to make delicious marinades and sauces. If you find it too greasy you can always reduce it in a saucepan to get rid of the excess liquid.

• Cleaning both the basket and drawer after every use is imperative.

Now that you've gotten to know the basics of using the air fryer, let's get to the exciting part—it's cooking time!

BREAKFAST

Banana Bread

Preparation Time: 10 minutes

Cooking time: 20 minutes

Servings: 8

INGREDIENTS:

- 1 1/3 cups flour

- 1 teaspoon baking soda 1 teaspoon baking powder

- . cup milk

- 3 bananas, peeled and sliced

- 2/3 cup sugar

- 1 teaspoon ground cinnamon

- 1 teaspoon salt

- . cup olive oil

DIRECTIONS:

1. Preheat the Air fryer to 330 o F and grease a loaf pan.

2. Mix together all the dry ingredients with the wet ingredients to form a dough.

3. Place the dough into the prepared loaf pan and transfer into an air fryer basket.

4. Cook for about 20 minutes and remove from air fryer.

5. Cut the bread into desired size slices and serve warm.

NUTRITION:

Calories:295,Fat:13.3g, Carbohydrates: 44g, Sugar: 22.8g, Protein: 3.1g, Sodium: 458mg

Flavorful Bacon Cups

Preparation Time: 10 minutes

Cooking time: 15 minutes

Servings: 6

INGREDIENTS:

• 6 bacon slices

• 6 bread slices

• 1 scallion, chopped

• 3 tablespoons green bell pepper,

seeded and chopped

• 6 eggs

• 2 tablespoons low-fat mayonnaise

DIRECTIONS:

1. Preheat the Air fryer to 375 o F and grease 6 cups muffin tin with cooking spray.

2. Place each bacon slice in a prepared muffin cup.

3. Cut the bread slices with round cookie cutter and place over the bacon slices.

4. Top with bell pepper, scallion and mayonnaise evenly and crack 1 egg in each muffin cup.

5. Place in the Air fryer and cook for about 15 minutes.

6. Dish out and serve warm.

NUTRITION:

Calories: 260, Fat: 18g, Carbohydrates: 6.9g, Sugar: 1.03g, Protein: 16.7g, Sodium: 805mg

Breakfast Bacon Hash

Preparation time: 10 minutes

Cooking time: 18minutes

Servings: 6

INGREDIENTS

- 1 cup kale
- 3 eggs
- 2 oz bacon, chopped, cooked
- 1 sweet potato, grated
- ½ teaspoon thyme
- ½ teaspoon ground black pepper
- ½ teaspoon ground paprika
- ½ cup coconut milk
- 1 onion, chopped
- 1 teaspoon olive oil

DIRECTIONS

1. Chop the kale roughly and place it in the blender.

2. Blend it gently.

3. Then transfer the blended kale in the mixing bowl.

4. Add the grated potato and thyme.

5.   Sprinkle the mixture with the ground black pepper and ground paprika.

6.   Add   coconut   milk and   chopped onion.

7.   Pour the olive oil into the air fryer basket.

8.   Then place the kale mixture in the air fryer basket,

9.   Beat the eggs in the separate bowl and whisk well.

11.   Pour the whisked eggs over the kale mixture.

12.   Cook the quiche for 18 minutes at 350 F.

13.   When the time is over – chill the quiche little and serve

Spaghetti Squash Casserole Cups

Preparation time: 10 minutes

Cooking time: 19 minutes

Servings: 2

INGREDIENTS

* 1 oz bacon, chopped
* 1 carrot
* 1 apple
* 1 teaspoon olive oil
* ½ teaspoon salt
* ¼ teaspoon thyme

DIRECTIONS

1. Put the chopped bacon in the air fryer basket.
2. Add salt and stir it gently.
3. Cook the bacon for 4 minutes at 365 F.
4. Peel the carrot and grate it.
5. Add the grated carrot.
6. Then grate the apple and add the carrot mixture too.
7. Stir it carefully.

8.   Sprinkle the bacon hash with the thyme and stir gently again.

9.   Cook the bacon hash for 15 minutes at 365 F.

10.   Stir it carefully and serve!

NUTRITION:

Calories 168, Fat 8.5, Fiber 3.5, Carbs 18.7, Protein 5.8

MAINS

Buttery Cod Bake

Preparation Time: 17 minutes

Servings: 4

INGREDIENTS:

• 2 cod fillets, boneless, skinless and cubed • . cup tomato sauce

• 8 cherry tomatoes; halved

• 3 tbsp. butter; melted

• 2 tbsp. parsley; chopped.

• Salt and black pepper to taste.

DIRECTIONS:

1. In a baking pan that fits the air fryer, combine all the ingredients, toss, put the pan in the machine and cook the mix at 390°F for 12 minutes

2. Divide the mix into bowls and serve for lunch.

NUTRITION:

Calories: 232; Fat: 8g; Fiber: 2g; Carbs: 5g; Protein: 11g

Broccoli Stew

Preparation Time: 20 minutes

Servings: 4

INGREDIENTS:

• 1 broccoli head, florets separated

• . cup celery; chopped.

• . cup tomato sauce

• 3 spring onions; chopped.

• 3 tbsp. chicken stock

• Salt and black pepper to taste.

DIRECTIONS:

1. In a pan that fits your air fryer, mix all the ingredients, toss, introduce the pan in your fryer and cook at 380°F for 15 minutes

2. Divide into bowls and serve for lunch.

NUTRITION:

Calories: 183; Fat: 4g; Fiber: 2g; Carbs: 4g; Protein: 7g

Tomato and Cranberry Beans Pasta

Preparation time: 10 minutes

Cooking time: 15 minutes Servings: 8

INGREDIENTS

- 2cups canned cranberry beans, drained

- 2celery ribs, chopped

- 1yellow onion, chopped

- 7garlic cloves, minced

- 1teaspoon rosemary, chopped

- 26ounces canned tomatoes, chopped

- ¼ teaspoon red pepper flakes

- 2teaspoons oregano, dried

- 3teaspoons basil, dried

- ½ teaspoon smoked paprika

- A pinch of salt and black pepper

- 10ounces kale, roughly chopped

- 2cups whole wheat vegan pasta, cooked

DIRECTIONS

1. In a pan that fits your air fryer, combine beans with celery, onion, garlic, rosemary, tomatoes, pepper flakes, oregano, basil, paprika, salt, pepper and kale, introduce in your air fryer and cook at 365 degrees F for 15 minutes.

2. Divide vegan pasta between plates, add cranberry mix on top and serve.

3. Enjoy!

NUTRITION:

Calories 251, Fat 2, Fiber 12, Carbs 12, Protein 6

Mexican Casserole

Preparation time: 10 minutes

Cooking time: 15 minutes Servings: 4

INGREDIENTS

- 1 tablespoon olive oil

- 4 garlic cloves, minced

- 1 yellow onion, chopped

- 2 tablespoons cilantro, chopped

- 1 small red chili, chopped

- 2 teaspoons cumin, ground

- Salt and black pepper to the taste

- 1 teaspoon sweet paprika

- 1 teaspoon coriander seeds

- 1 pound sweet potatoes, cubed

- Juice of ½ lime

- 10ounces green beans

- 2cups tomatoes, chopped

- 1tablespoon parsley, chopped

DIRECTIONS

1. Grease a pan that fits your air fryer with the oil, add garlic, onion, cilantro, red chili, cumin, salt, pepper, paprika, coriander, potatoes, lime juice, green beans and tomatoes, toss, place in your air fryer and cook at 365 degrees F for 15 minutes.

2. Add parsley, divide between plates and serve.

3. Enjoy!

NUTRITION: Calories 223, Fat 5, Fiber 4, Carbs 7, Protein 8

SIDES

Minty Peas

Preparation time: 5 minutes

Cooking time: 12 minutes

Servings: 4

INGREDIENTS:

- 1 pound fresh peas

- 1 green onion, sliced

- 1 tablespoon mint, chopped

- . cup veggie stock

- 1 tablespoon butter, melted

- Salt and black pepper to taste

DIRECTIONS:

1. Place all of the ingredients into a pan that fits your air fryer and mix well.

2. Put the pan in the air fryer and cook at 370 degrees F for 12 minutes.

3. Divide between plates and serve.

NUTRITION:

calories 151, fat 2, fiber 6, carbs 9, protein 5

Lemony Artichokes

Preparation time: 10 minutes

Cooking time: 25 minutes

Servings: 4

INGREDIENTS:

• 2 medium artichokes, trimmed

• Juice of . lemon

• A drizzle of olive oil

• Salt to taste

DIRECTIONS:

1. Brush the artichokes with the oil, season with salt, and put them in your air fryer's basket.

2. Cook at 370 degrees F for 20 minutes.

3. Divide between plates, drizzle lemon juice all over, and serve.

NUTRITION:calories 151, fat 3, fiber 7, carbs 8, protein 4

Citrus Cauliflower Mix

Preparation time: 5 minutes

Cooking time: 14 minutes

Servings: 4

INGREDIENTS:

• 2 small cauliflower heads, florets separated

• Juice of 1 orange

• A pinch of hot pepper flakes

• Salt and black pepper to taste

• 4 tablespoons olive oil

DIRECTIONS:

1. Brush the cauliflower with the oil, then season with salt, pepper, and the pepper flakes.

2. Transfer the cauliflower to your air fryer's basket and cook at 380 degrees F for 14 minutes.

3. Divide between plates, drizzle orange juice all over, and serve.

NUTRITION:

calories 151, fat 7, fiber 4, carbs 9, protein 4

Spicy Mozzarella Stick

Cooking Time: 5 minutes

Servings: 3

INGREDIENTS

- 8-ounces mozzarella cheese, cut into strips

- 2tablespoons olive oil

- ½ teaspoon salt

- 1cup pork rinds

- 1egg

- 1teaspoon garlic powder

- 1teaspoon paprika

DIRECTIONS

1. Cut the mozzarella into 6 strips. Whisk the egg along with salt, paprika, and garlic powder. Dip the mozzarella strips into egg mixture first, then into

2. pork rinds.

3. Arrange them on a baking platter and place in the fridge for 30- minutes. Preheat your air fryer to 360°Fahrenheit.

4. Drizzle olive oil into the air fryer. Arrange the mozzarella sticks in

5. the air fryer and cook for about 5- minutes. Make sure to turn them at least twice, to ensure they will become golden on all sides.

NUTRITION:

Calories: 156, Total Fat: 9.6g, Carbs: 1.89g, Protein: 16g

SEAFOOD

Juicy Salmon and Asparagus Parcels

Preparation Time: 5 minutes

Cooking time: 13 minutes

Servings: 2

INGREDIENTS:

- 2 salmon fillets

- 4 asparagus stalks

- . cup champagne

- Salt and black pepper, to taste

- . cup white sauce

- 1 teaspoon olive oil

DIRECTIONS:

1. Preheat the Air fryer to 355 o F and grease an Air fryer basket.

2. Mix all the ingredients in a bowl and divide this mixture evenly over

2 foil papers.

3. Arrange the foil papers in the Air fryer basket and cook for about 13

minutes.

4. Dish out in a platter and serve hot.

NUTRITION:

Calories: 328, Fat: 16.6g, Carbohydrates:

4.1g, Sugar: 1.8g, Protein: 36.6g, Sodium: 190mg

Appetizing Tuna Patties

Preparation Time: 15 minutes

Cooking time: 10 minutes

Servings: 6

INGREDIENTS:

• 2, 6-ouncecans tuna, drained

• . cup panko bread crumbs

• 1 egg

• 2 tablespoons fresh parsley, chopped

• 2 teaspoons Dijon mustard Dash of Tabasco sauce

• 1 tablespoon fresh lemon juice

• 1 tablespoon olive oil

DIRECTIONS:

1. Preheat the Air fryer to 355 o F and line a baking tray with foil paper.

2. Mix all the ingredients in a large bowl until well combined.

3. Make equal sized patties from the mixture and refrigerate overnight.

4. Arrange the patties on the baking tray and transfer to an Air fryer basket.

5. Cook for about 10 minutes and dish out to serve warm.

NUTRITION:

Calories: 130, Fat: 6.2g, Carbohydrates: 5.1g, Sugar: 0.5g, Protein: 13g, Sodium: 94mg

Quick and Easy Shrimp

Preparation Time: 10 minutes

Cooking time: 5 minutes

Servings: 2

INGREDIENTS:

- . pound tiger shrimp

- 1 tablespoon olive oil

- . teaspoon old bay seasoning

- . teaspoon smoked paprika

- . teaspoon cayenne pepper

- Salt, to taste

DIRECTIONS:

1. Preheat the Air fryer to 390 o F and grease an Air fryer basket.

2. Mix all the ingredients in a large bowlb until well combined.

3. Place the shrimps in the Air fryer basket and cook for about 5 minutes.

4. Dish out and serve warm.

NUTRITION:

Calories: 174, Fat: 8.3g, Carbohydrates: 0.3g, Sugar: 0g, Protein: 23.8g, Sodium: 492mg

Trout and Red Chili Mix

Preparation time: 10 minutes

Cooking time: 15minutes

Servings: 4

INGREDIENTS

- 4trout fillets, boneless

- Salt and black pepper to the taste

- 1red chili pepper, chopped

- 1green chili pepper, chopped

- 1cup heavy cream

- 1tablespoon lemon juice

DIRECTIONS

1. In the air fryer's pan, mix the fish with the chilies and the other ingredients, toss, cook at 360 degrees F for 15 minutes, divide between plates and serve.

NUTRITION:

Calories 271, Fat 4, Fiber 2, Carbs 15, Protein 11

POULTRY

Chicken and Green Onions Stir Fry Recipe

Preparation Time: 26 Minutes

Servings: 4

INGREDIENTS:

• chopped piece ginger root-1-inch

• Fish sauce-2 tbsp.

• Soy sauce-3 tbsp.

• minced garlic cloves; -4

• Chinese five spice-1 tsp.

• chicken drumsticks-10

• Melted butter-1 tsp.

• roughly chopped green onions -10

• Coconut milk-1 cup

• lime juice-1 tbsp.

• chopped cilantro-1/4 cup

• Salt and black pepper to the taste

DIRECTIONS

1. Mix green onions with ginger, garlic, soy sauce, fish sauce, five zest, salt, pepper, spread and coconut milk In your sustenance processor and heartbeat the blend well.

2. Mix chicken with green onions blend In a bowl and hurl appropriately,

3. Move everything to a container that accommodates your air fryer and cook at 370 °F, for 16 minutes; shaking the fryer once.

4. Share among plates at that point sprinkle cilantro on top, and shower

lime squeeze everywhere

5. Serve dinner with a side plate of mixed greens.

NUTRITION:

Calories: 321; Fat: 12; Fiber: 12; Carbs: 22; Protein: 20

Special Chicken Cacciatore Recipe

Preparation Time: 30 Minutes

Serves:4

INGREDIENTS:

- 8 chicken drumsticks; bone-in

- pitted and sliced black olives-1/2 cup

- bay leaf-1

- Garlic powder-1 tsp.

- chopped yellow onion-1

- Crushed canned tomatoes and juice - 28 oz.

- Dried oregano-1 tsp.

- Salt and black pepper to the taste

DIRECTIONS:

1. Mix chicken with salt, pepper, garlic powder, sound leaf, onion, tomatoes and juice, oregano and olives in a protected dish that fits into your air fryer; hurl the whole blend. air fryer and cook at 365 °F, for 20 minutes.

3. Share dish among plates and serve hot.

NUTRITION:

Calories: 300; Fiber: 8; Fat: 12; Carbs: 20; Protein:

Maple Chicken Mix

Preparation time: 10 minutes

Cooking time: 30 minutes

Servings: 4

INGREDIENTS

- 2pounds chicken breast, skinless, boneless and cubed

- 2tablespoons maple syrup

- Salt and black pepper to the taste

- 4spring onions, chopped

- 2tablespoons olive oil

DIRECTIONS

1. In the air fryer's basket, mix the chicken with the maple syrup and the other ingredients, toss cook at

360 degrees F for 30 minutes, divide between plates and serve.

NUTRITION:

Calories 271, Fat 8, Fiber 12, Carbs 26, Protein 17

Whole Chicken Mix

Preparation time: 10 minutes

Cooking time: 35 minutes

Servings: 8

INGREDIENTS

- 1-2 pounds whole chicken, cut into medium pieces

- 3tablespoons olive oil

- 1cup chicken stock

- ½ teaspoon sweet paprika

- 1tablespoon ginger, grated

- Salt and black pepper to the taste

DIRECTIONS

1. In the air fryer's basket, mix the whole chicken with the oil and the other ingredients, rub and cook at 380 degrees F for 35 minutes.

2.   Divide between plates and serve with a side salad.

NUTRITION:

Calories 220, Fat 10, Fiber 8, Carbs 20, Protein 16

MEAT

Seared Ribeye

Preparation Time: 50 minutes Servings: 2

INGREDIENTS:

- 1, 8-oz.ribeye steak

- 1 tbsp. salted butter; softened.

- 1 tbsp. coconut oil

- . tsp. dried parsley.

- . tsp. pink Himalayan salt

- . tsp. ground peppercorn

- . tsp. dried oregano.

- . tsp. garlic powder.

DIRECTIONS:

1. Rub steak with salt and ground peppercorn. Place into the air fryer basket.

2. Adjust the temperature to 250 Degrees F and set the timer for 45 minutes.

3. After timer beeps, begin checking doneness and add a few minutes until internal temperature is your personal preference

4. In a medium skillet over medium heat, add coconut oil. When oil is hot,quickly sear outside and sides of steak until crisp and browned. Remove from heat and allow steak to rest

5. In a small bowl, whip butter with garlic powder, parsley and oregano. Slice steak and serve with herb butter on top.

NUTRITION:

Calories: 377;

Lasagna Casserole

Preparation Time: 30 minutes

Servings: 4

INGREDIENTS:

- . cup low-carb no-sugar-added pasta sauce

- 1 lb. 80/20 ground beef; cooke and drained

- . cup full-fat ricotta cheese

- . cup grated Parmesan cheese.

- . tsp. garlic powder.

- 1 tsp. dried parsley.

- . tsp. dried oregano.

- 1 cup shredded mozzarella cheese

DIRECTIONS:

1. In a 4-cup round baking dish, pour . cup pasta sauce on the bottom of the dish. Place . of the ground beef on top of the sauce.

2. In a small bowl, mix ricotta, Parmesan, garlic powder, parsley and oregano. Place dollops of half the mixture on top of the beef

3. Sprinkle with ⅓ of the mozzarella. Repeat layers until all beef, ricotta mixture, sauce and mozzarella are used, ending with the mozzarella on top

4. Cover dish with foil and place into the air fryer basket. Adjust the temperature

to 370 Degrees F and set the timer for 15 minutes. In the last 2 minutes of cooking, remove the foil to brown the cheese. Serve immediately.

NUTRITION:

Calories: 371; Protein: 31.4g; Fiber: 1.6g; Fat: 21.4g; Carbs: 5.8g

Easy Pork Chops

Preparation Time: 25 minutes

Servings: 4

INGREDIENTS:

- 1. oz. pork rinds, finely ground

- 1 tsp. chili powder

- . tsp. garlic powder.

- 1 tbsp. coconut oil; melted

- 4, 4-oz.pork chops

DIRECTIONS:

1. Take a large bowl, mix ground pork rinds, chili powder and garlic powder.

2. Brush each pork chop with coconut oil and then press into the pork rind

mixture, coating both sides. Place each coated pork chop into the air fryer basket

3. Adjust the temperature to 400 Degrees F and set the timer for 15 minutes. Flip each pork chop halfway through the cooking time

4. When fully cooked the pork chops will be golden on the outside and have an internal temperature of at least 145 Degrees F.

NUTRITION:

Calories: 292; Protein: 29.5g; Fiber: 0.3g; Fat: 18.5g; Carbs: 0.6g

Chicken and Pineapple Mix

Preparation time: 10 minutes

Cooking time: 25 minutes

Servings: 4

INGREDIENTS

- 2pounds chicken breast, skinless, boneless and cubed

- 1cup pineapple, peeled and cubed

- 2tablespoons avocado oil

- 1tablespoon rosemary, chopped

- Salt and black pepper to the taste

- ½ teaspoon chili powder

- 2tablespoons honey

DIRECTIONS

1. In the air fryer's pan, mix the chicken with the pineapple and the other ingredients, toss, cook at

390 degrees F for 25 minutes, divide between plates and serve.

NUTRITION:

Calories 281, Fat 11, Fiber 12, Carbs 28, Protein 19

EGGS AND DAIRY

Vegetarian Tofu Scramble

Preparation Time: 15 minutes

Servings: 2

INGREDIENTS

- 1/2 teaspoon fresh lemon juice

- 1 teaspoon coarse salt

- 1 teaspoon coarse ground black pepper

- 4 ounces fresh spinach, chopped

- 1 tablespoon butter, melted

- 1/3 cup fresh basil, roughly chopped

- 1/2 teaspoon fresh lemon juice

- 13 ounces soft silken tofu, drained

DIRECTIONS

1. Add the tofu and olive oil to a baking dish.

2. Cook for 9 minutes at 272 degrees F.

3. Add the other ingredients and cook another 5 minutes. Serve warm.

NUTRITION:

232 Calories;

16.6g Fat;

5.8g Carbs;

19.9g Protein;

1.2g Sugars;

2g Fiber

Baked Eggs with Linguica Sausage

Preparation Time: 18 minutes

Servings: 2

INGREDIENTS

• 1/2 cup Cheddar cheese, shredded

• 4 eggs

• 2 ounces Linguica, Portuguese

pork sausage, chopped

• 1/2 onion, peeled and chopped

• 2 tablespoons olive oil

• 1/2 teaspoon rosemary, chopped

• . teaspoon marjoram

• 1/4 cup sour cream

• Sea salt and freshly ground black pepper, to taste

• . teaspoon fresh sage, chopped

DIRECTIONS

1. Lightly grease 2 oven safe ramekins with olive oil. Now, divide the sausage and onions among these ramekins.

2. Crack an egg into each ramekin; add the remaining items, minus the cheese. Airfry at 355 degrees F approximately 13 minutes.

3. Immediately top with Cheddar cheese, serve, and enjoy.

NUTRITION:

544 Calories; 45.1g Fat; 8.2g Carbs; 24.4g Protein; 4.2g Sugars; 0.9g Fiber

VEGETABLES

Chives Beets Mix

Preparation time: 10 minutes

Cooking time: 25 minutes

Servings: 4

INGREDIENTS:

• 4 beets, peeled and cut into wedges

• 2 tablespoons olive oil

• 1 tablespoon chives, chopped

• 2 garlic cloves, minced

• Salt and black pepper to the taste

• 1 teaspoon cumin, ground

DIRECTIONS:

1. In your air fryer's basket, combine the beets with the oil and the other ingredients, toss and cook at 380 degrees F for 25 minutes.

2. Divide the mix between plates and serve.

NUTRITION: calories 100, fat 2, fiber 4, carbs 7, protein 5

Kale Sauté

Preparation time: 10 minutes

Cooking time: 12 minutes

Servings: 4

INGREDIENTS:

- 1 pound baby kale
- 2 scallions, chopped
- 1 tablespoon olive oil
- 2 tablespoons balsamic vinegar
- . teaspoon chili powder
- 1 teaspoon coriander, ground
- Salt and black pepper to the taste

DIRECTIONS:

1. Heat up the air fryer with the oil at 370 degrees F, add the kale, scallions and the other ingredients, toss and cook for 12 minutes.

2. Divide the mix between plates and serve.

NUTRITION: calories 151, fat 2, fiber 3, carbs 9, protein 4

Avocado and Tomato Salad

Preparation time: 10minutes

Cooking time: 12 minutes

Servings: 4

INGREDIENTS:

• 1 pound tomatoes, cut into wedges

• 2 avocados, peeled, pitted and sliced

• 2 tablespoons avocado oil

• 1 red onion, sliced

• 1 tablespoon balsamic vinegar

• Salt and black pepper to the taste

• 1 tablespoon cilantro, chopped

DIRECTIONS:

1. In your air fryer, combine the tomatoes with the avocados and the other ingredients, toss and cook at 360 degrees F for 12 minutes.

2. Divide between plates and serve.

NUTRITION: calories 144, fat 7, fiber 5, carbs 8, protein 6

Salsa Zucchini

Preparation time: 5 minutes

Cooking time: 20 minutes

Servings: 4

INGREDIENTS

- 1pound zucchinis, roughly sliced

- 1cup mild salsa

- 1red onion, chopped

- Salt and black pepper to the taste

- 2tablespoons lime juice

- 2tablespoons olive oil

- 1teaspoon coriander, ground

DIRECTIONS

1. In a pan that fits your air fryer, mix the zucchinis with the salsa and the other ingredients, toss, introduce in the fryer and cook at 390 degrees F for 20 minutes.

2.   Divide the mix between plates and serve.

NUTRITION:

Calories 150, Fat 4, Fiber 2, Carbs 4, Protein 5

SNACKS

Olives Dip

Preparation Time: 10 minutes

Servings: 6

INGREDIENTS:

- 1 cup black olives, pitted and chopped.

- . cup capers

- . cup olive oil

- 1 cup parsley leaves

- 1 cup basil leaves

- 2 garlic cloves; minced

- 3 tbsp. lemon juice

- 2 tsp. apple cider vinegar

- A pinch of salt and black pepper

DIRECTIONS:

1. In a blender, combine all the ingredients, pulse well and transfer to a ramekin.

2. Place the ramekin in your air fryer's basket and cook at 350°F for 5 minutes

NUTRITION:

Calories: 120

Parmesan Chicken Wings

Preparation Time: 30 minutes

Servings: 4

INGREDIENTS:

• 2 lb. raw chicken wings

• ⅓ cup grated Parmesan cheese.

• 1 tbsp. baking powder

• 4 tbsp. unsalted butter; melted.

• . tsp. dried parsley.

• . tsp. garlic powder.

• 1 tsp. pink Himalayan salt

DIRECTIONS:

1. Take a large bowl, place chicken wings, salt, . tsp. garlic powder. and baking

powder, then toss. Place wings into the air fryer basket

2. Adjust the temperature to 400 Degrees F and set the timer for 25 minutes. Toss the basket two or three times during the cooking time

3. In a small bowl, combine butter, Parmesan and parsley.

4. Remove wings from the fryer and place into a clean large bowl. Pour the butter mixture over the wings and toss until coated. Serve warm.

NUTRITION:

Calories: 565; Protein: 41.8g; Fiber: 0.1g; Fat: 42.1g; Carbs: 2.2g

Cheese Bread

Preparation Time: 20 minutes

Servings: 2

INGREDIENTS:

- . cup grated Parmesan cheese.

- 1 cup shredded mozzarella cheese

- 1 large egg.

- . tsp. garlic powder.

DIRECTIONS:

1. Mix all ingredients in a large bowl. Cut a piece of parchment to fit your air fryer

basket. Press the mixture into a circle on the parchment and place into the air fryer basket

2. Adjust the temperature to 350 Degrees F and set the timer for 10 minutes.

NUTRITION: Calories: 258; Protein: 19.2g; Fiber: 0.1g; Fat: 16.6g; Carbs: 3.7g

Ginger Cookies Cheesecake

Preparation time: 15 minutes

Cooking time: 15 minutes

Servings: 6

INGREDIENTS

- 2cups water, for the pressure cooker

- 2teaspoons butter, melted

- ½ cup ginger cookies, crumbled

- 16ounces cream cheese, soft

- 2eggs

- ½ cup sugar

DIRECTIONS

1.   Grease a cake pan with the butter, add cookie crumbs and spread them evenly.

2.   In a bowl, beat cream cheese with a mixer.

3.   Add eggs and sugar and stir very well.

4.	Add the water to your pressure cooker, add steamer basket, add cake pan inside, cover and cook on High for 15 minutes.

5.	Keep cheesecake in the fridge for a few hours before serving it.

NUTRITION:

Calories 394, Fat 12, Fiber 3, Carbs 20

Winter Cherry Mix

Preparation time: 10 minutes

Cooking time: 5 minutes

Servings: 6

INGREDIENTS

- 16ounces cherries, pitted

- 2tablespoons water

- 2tablespoons lemon juice

- Sugar to the taste

- 2tablespoons cornstarch

DIRECTIONS

1. In your pressure cooker, mix cherries with sugar and lemon juice, stir, cover and cook on High for 3 minutes.

2. In a bowl, mix water with cornstarch, stir well, add to the pot, set the cooker on sauté mode, add the rest of the cherries, stir, cook for 2 minutes, divide into bowls and serve cold.

NUTRITION: Calories 161, Fat 4, Fiber 2, Carbs 8, Protein

DESSERTS

Avocado Granola

Preparation Time: 12 minutes

Servings: 6

INGREDIENTS:

• 1 cup avocado, peeled, pitted and cubed

• . cup walnuts; chopped.

• . cup almonds; chopped.

• . cup coconut flakes

• 2 tbsp. stevia

• 2 tbsp. ghee; melted

DIRECTIONS:

1. In a pan that fits your air fryer, mix all the ingredients, toss, put the pan in the fryer and cook at 320°F for 8 minutes

2. Divide into bowls and serve right away.

NUTRITION:

Calories: 170; Fat: 3g; Fiber: 2g; Carbs: 4g; Protein: 3g

Cocoa and Nuts Bombs

Preparation Time: 13 minutes

Servings: 12

INGREDIENTS:

• 2 cups macadamia nuts; chopped.

• . cup cocoa powder

• 1/3 cup swerve

• 4 tbsp. coconut oil; melted

• 1 tsp. vanilla extract

DIRECTIONS:

1. Take a bowl and mix all the ingredients and whisk well.

2. Shape medium balls out of this mix,place them in your air fryer and cook at 300°F for 8 minutes. Serve cold

NUTRITION:

Calories: 120; Fat: 12g; Fiber: 1g; Carbs: 2g; Protein: 1g

Banana Cake

Preparation time: 10 minutes

Cooking time: 1 hour

Servings: 4

INGREDIENTS

- 1cup water, for the pressure cooker

- 1and ½ cups sugar

- 2cups flour

- 4bananas, peeled and mashed

- 1teaspoon cinnamon powder

- 1teaspoon nutmeg powder

DIRECTIONS

1. In a bowl, mix sugar with flour, bananas, cinnamon and nutmeg, stir, pour into a greased cake pan and cover with tin foil.

2.   Add the water to your pressure cooker, add steamer basket, add cake pan, cover and cook on High for 1 hour.

3.   Slice, divide between plates and serve cold.

4.   NUTRITION:

Calories 300, Fat 10, Fiber 4, Carbs 45

Pineapple Pudding

Preparation time: 10 minutes

Cooking time: 5 minutes

Servings: 8

INGREDIENTS

- 1tablespoon avocado oil

- 1cup rice

- 14ounces milk

- Sugar to the taste

- 8ounces canned pineapple, chopped

DIRECTIONS

1. In your pressure cooker, mix oil, milk and rice, stir, cover and cook on High for 3 minutes.

2. Add sugar and pineapple, stir, cover and cook on High for 2 minutes more.

3. Divide into dessert bowls and serve.

NUTRITION: Calories 154, Fat 4, Fiber 1, Carbs 14

Blueberry Jam

Preparation time: 10 minutes

Cooking time: 11 minutes

Servings: 2

INGREDIENTS

- ½ pound blueberries

- 1/3 pound sugar

- Zest from ½ lemon, grated

- ½ tablespoon butter

- A pinch of cinnamon powder

DIRECTIONS

1.   Put the blueberries in your blender, pulse them well, strain, transfer to your pressure cooker, add sugar, lemon zest and cinnamon, stir, cover and simmer on sauté mode for 3 minutes.

2.   Add butter, stir, cover the cooker and cook on High for 8 minutes.

3.   Transfer to a jar and serve.

NUTRITION:

Calories 211, Fat 3, Fiber 3, Carbs 6,